Timber Rattlesnakes

by J. Clark Sawyer

Consultant: Professor Harry W. Greene
Department of Ecology and Evolutionary Biology
Cornell University
Ithaca, New York

BEARPORT PUBLISHING

New York, New York

Credits

Cover and Title Page, © Evin T Carter/Shutterstock; TOC, © Eric Isselee/Shutterstock;
4–5, © George Grall/Getty Images; 6–7, © Leszczynski, Zigmund/Animals Animals/Earth Scenes;
7, © Chas. & Elizabeth Schwartz Trust/Animals Animals/Earth Scenes; 8–9, © Pete Oxford/
naturepl; 10–11, © Matthew Jennette; 11, © John M. Burnley/Science Photo Library;
12, © age fotostock/SuperStock; 13, © John Cancalosi/Alamy; 14–15, © Matthew Ignoffo;
16–17, © Jim Scharosch, herpjournal.com; 18–19, © John Cancalosi/National Geographic
Society/Corbis; 20–21, © Joe McDonald/Corbis; 22T, © Eric Isselee/Shutterstock;
22B, © Chamelion Studio/Shutterstock; 23TL, © Chas. & Elizabeth Schwartz Trust/Animals
Animals/Earth Scenes; 23TR, © John M. Burnley/Science Photo Library; 23BL, © iStockphoto/
Thinkstock; 23BR, © Leszczynski, Zigmund/Animals Animals/Earth Scenes.

Publisher: Kenn Goin
Editor: Jessica Rudolph
Creative Director: Spencer Brinker
Design: Debrah Kaiser
Photo Researcher: Michael Win

Library of Congress Cataloging-in-Publication Data

Clark Sawyer, J., author.
  Timber rattlesnakes / by J. Clark Sawyer.
     pages cm. — (In winter, where do they go?)
  Includes bibliographical references and index.
  ISBN-13: 978-1-62724-318-6 (library binding)
  ISBN-10: 1-62724-318-6 (library binding)
  1. Timber rattlesnake—Juvenile literature. 2. Rattlesnakes—Juvenile literature. I. Title.
  QL666.O69C58 2015
  597.96'38—dc23
                                    2014009029

For more information, write to Bearport Publishing Company, Inc., 45 West 21st Street,
Suite 3B, New York, New York 10010. Printed in the United States of America.

10 9 8 7 6 5 4 3 2 1

Contents

Timber Rattlesnakes

It's a fall day in a forest.

A timber rattlesnake is coiled on top of some leaves.

It waits to catch a meal.

Timber rattlers can be yellow, gray, or other colors. They all have dark bands.

A tiny mouse runs by.

The snake strikes.

Venom from its bite kills the mouse.

The snake swallows it whole.

Rattlers use sharp teeth called **fangs** to bite animals. Deadly venom shoots out of the fangs.

fangs

7

Soon, winter will come.

The snake slithers into its den.

The den is a small hole under the ground.

Dens protect snakes from the cold.

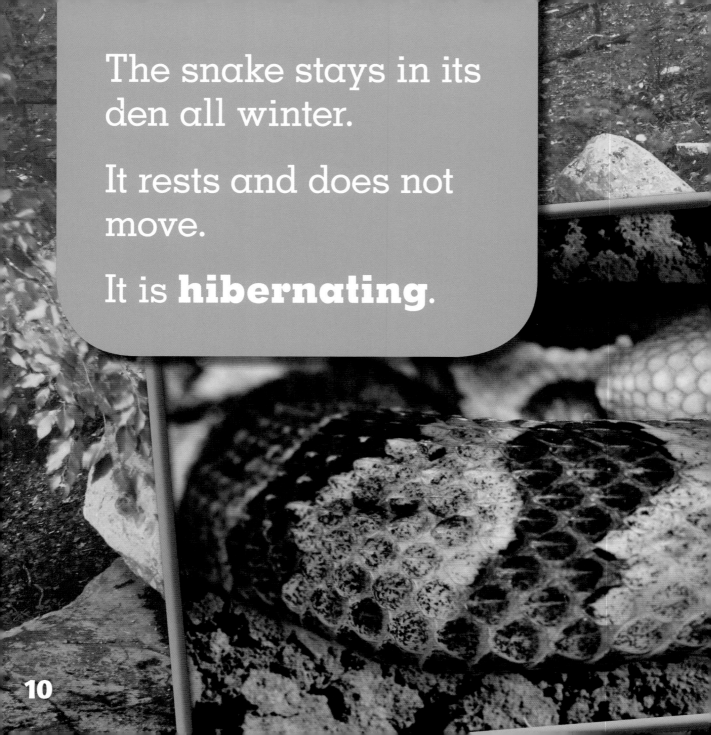

The snake stays in its den all winter.

It rests and does not move.

It is **hibernating**.

10

Other animals also hibernate. For example, some kinds of bats hibernate in caves.

bats

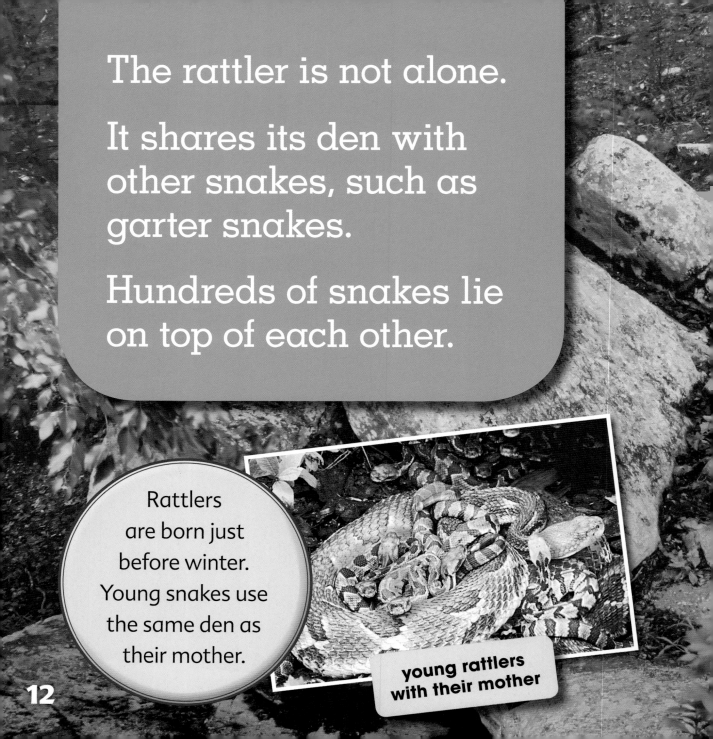

The rattler is not alone.

It shares its den with other snakes, such as garter snakes.

Hundreds of snakes lie on top of each other.

Rattlers are born just before winter. Young snakes use the same den as their mother.

young rattlers with their mother

Snakes' Den

In its den, the snake does not eat.

It also does not drink.

Rattlers hibernate for up to seven months.

In spring, the weather becomes warmer.

The snake leaves its den.

Rattlers usually use the same den year after year.

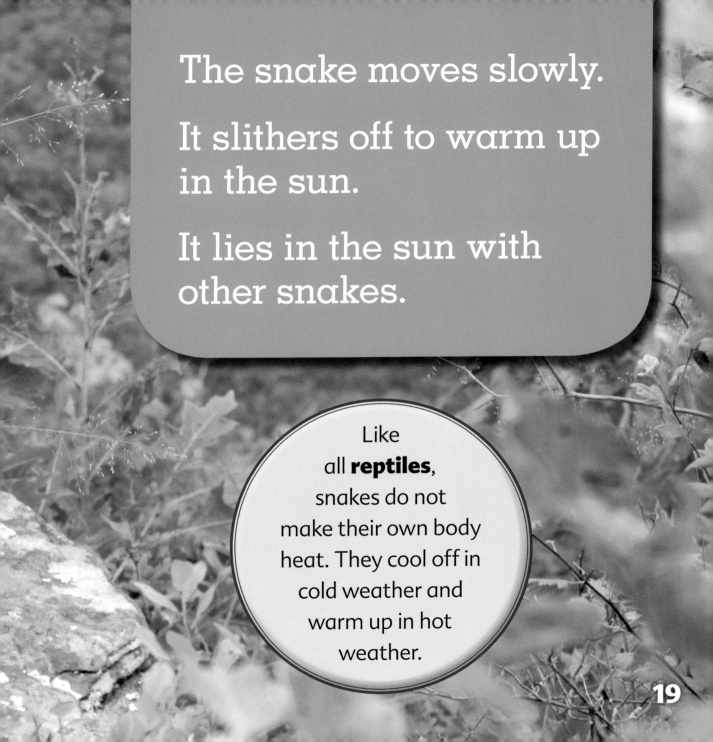

The snake moves slowly.

It slithers off to warm up in the sun.

It lies in the sun with other snakes.

Like all **reptiles**, snakes do not make their own body heat. They cool off in cold weather and warm up in hot weather.

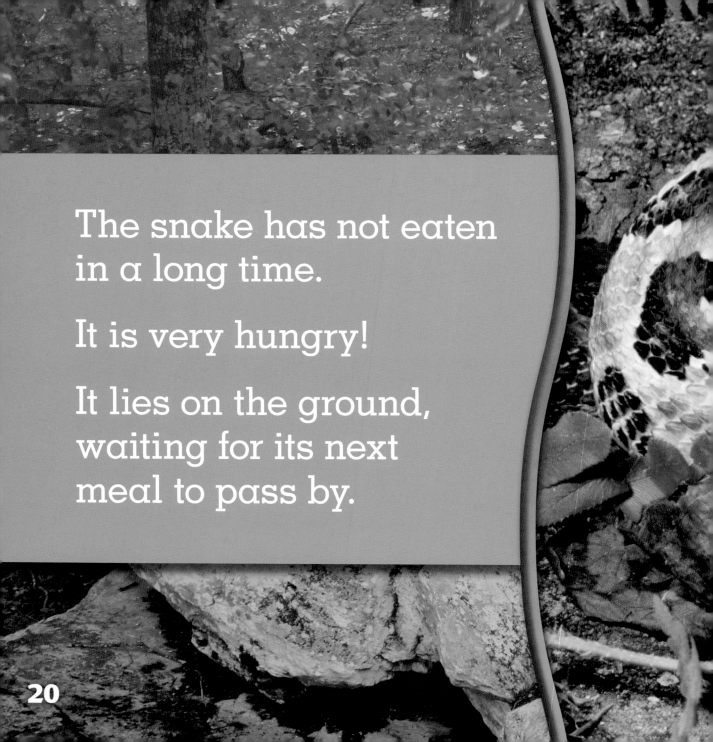

The snake has not eaten in a long time.

It is very hungry!

It lies on the ground, waiting for its next meal to pass by.

Timber rattlers live in dens only in the winter. When it's warm, they rest on rocks, grass, or leaves.

Timber Rattlesnake Facts

There are more than 30 kinds of rattlesnakes. Timber rattlers usually live in rocky areas in forests. They shake their tails when enemies, such as coyotes, get close. The rattling noise warns animals that the snakes may bite.

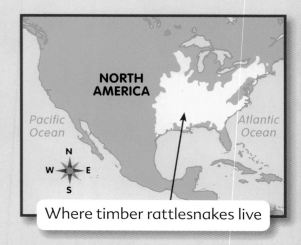

NORTH AMERICA

Pacific Ocean

Atlantic Ocean

N W E S

Where timber rattlesnakes live

Food: Mice, chipmunks, squirrels, rabbits, small birds, and frogs

Length: 3 to 5 feet (0.9 to 1.5 m)

Weight: 1.3 to 2 pounds (0.6 to 0.9 kg)

Life Span: About 20 years

Cool Fact: A timber rattlesnake's venom can kill a person if the bite isn't treated right away. However, rattlers rarely bite people. They usually try to hide if a person comes near.

Size of an adult timber rattlesnake

A teacup

Glossary

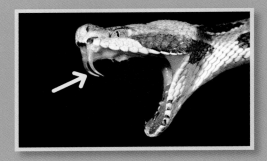

fangs (FANGZ) sharp, pointed teeth that some snakes use to pump venom into animals

hibernating (HYE-bur-*nayt*-ing) spending the winter in a cold, inactive state

reptiles (REP-tilez) animals, such as snakes and lizards, that have lungs for breathing, dry scaly skin, and backbones

venom (VEN-uhm) poison made by some snakes to kill animals

Index

Read More

Jackson, Kate. *Katie of the Sonoran Desert.* Tucson, AZ: Arizona-Sonora Desert Museum Press (2009).

White, Nancy. *Diamondback Rattlers: America's Most Venomous Snakes! (Fangs).* New York: Bearport (2009).

Learn More Online

To learn more about timber rattlesnakes, visit
www.bearportpublishing.com/InWinterWhereDoTheyGo?

About the Author

J. Clark Sawyer lives in Connecticut. She has edited and written many books about history, science, and nature for children.